"Sober Success: Climbing the Career Ladder Without a Liquid Safety Net,"

"A Hilarious and Practical Guide for Professionals Navigating Sobriety in the Workplace"

About the Author:

Lydia Wiggins, 57, is living proof that you can trade in your wine glasses for reading glasses and still have a blast. A specialist addiction counselor, NLP life coach, and online counseling guru, Lydia has swapped 15 years of active addiction for 6 years of active sobriety (and counting!).

When she's not busy being a supermom to 3 or a cool grandma (she prefers "Glam-ma"), Lydia can be found in South Africa, where the wildlife is wild and the Wi-Fi is... well, let's just say her online practice has made her an expert in the "Have you tried turning it off and on again?" method of tech support.

Lydia's journey from the bottom of the bottle to the top of her game has equipped her with a unique blend of professional expertise and been-there-done-that wisdom. She's like the GPS for your sobriety journey – but instead of "recalculating" when you make a wrong turn, she'll help you find a scenic detour to success.

With a wit sharper than a corkscrew and advice more refreshing than a virgin mojito, Lydia is here to show you that climbing the career ladder is a lot easier (and a lot more fun) when you're not wearing beer goggles.

So grab a copy of this book, a tall glass of your favorite non-alcoholic beverage, and get ready to laugh, learn, and level up your sober professional game. After all, as Lydia always says, "The only thing we're addicted to now is success... and maybe the occasional cat video."

Lydia Wiggins email: lydiawiggins3105@gmail.com whatsapp: +27736689301

CONTENTS:

Introduction: Sobering Up to Success

Chapter 1:

Understanding Addiction in the Workplace

Chapter 2:

Building a Strong Foundation for Sobriety

Chapter 3:

Navigating Professional Social Situations

Chapter 4:

Disclosure and Privacy

Chapter 5:

Stress Management for Sober Professionals

Chapter 6:

Career Advancement While Maintaining Sobriety

Chapter 7:

Handling Setbacks and Challenges

Chapter 8:

Technology and Tools for Sober Professionals

Chapter 9:

Physical and Mental Health for Career Success

Chapter 10:

Long-term Career Planning for Sober Professionals

Chapter 11:

Conclusion Chapter

Chapter 12:

Sobering Tales of Triumph

Chapter 13: THE 12 STEPS: Your career sobriety roadmap

Maintaining Sobriety While Advancing Your Career: A Professional's Guide

Introduction: Sobering Up to Success

Welcome, fellow professional! If you're reading this, you've likely already taken the courageous step of embracing sobriety. First off, give yourself a pat on the back—or better yet, treat yourself to that fancy ergonomic chair you've been eyeing. You deserve it!

Now, you might be thinking, "Great, I'm sober. But how on earth do I navigate the cutthroat world of business without the liquid courage I once relied on?" Fear not, my ambitious friend. This book is your new secret weapon, your personal career coach, and your sober cheerleader all rolled into one.

In the pages that follow, we'll tackle everything from surviving networking events without a cocktail in hand (spoiler alert: sparkling water is your new best friend) to climbing the corporate ladder without stepping on your sobriety. We'll laugh, we might cry (but blame it on the onions in the break room), and most importantly, we'll grow together.

Remember, you're not alone in this journey. Thousands of professionals are out there, crushing their career goals and maintaining their sobriety. And if they can do it, so can you—probably even better, because you have this book!

So, buckle up, grab your favourite non-alcoholic beverage, and let's embark on this adventure of professional growth and personal triumph. Trust me, your future sober, successful self will thank you.

Chapter 1:

Understanding Addiction in the Workplace (Or, Why Your Desk Plant Isn't a Suitable Drinking Buddy)

Picture this: It's 5 PM on a Friday. The office is buzzing with weekend plans, and there's talk of happy hour at the local watering hole. Your palms are sweaty, your mouth is dry, and you're wondering if anyone would notice if you made a swift exit through the fire escape.

Welcome to the wild world of navigating sobriety in a professional setting. It's like trying to play chess while everyone else is playing beer pong. But fear not! By the end of this chapter, you'll be the grandmaster of sober strategizing.

The Sneaky Triggers Lurking in Your Cubicle

First things first, let's talk triggers. In the professional world, they're everywhere. That stress-inducing email from your boss? Trigger. The celebration of landing a big client? Trigger. The mind-numbing boredom of yet another PowerPoint presentation? You guessed it—trigger.

But here's the thing: recognizing these triggers is half the battle. The other half is realizing that Karen from accounting's homemade kombucha is not an acceptable alternative.

Stress: The Ultimate Frenemy

Ah, work stress. It's like that clingy ex who just won't take the hint. In the past, you might have turned to alcohol to cope. Now, you're left wondering how to deal with deadline pressures without your old liquid crutch.

Here's a revolutionary idea: what if—and bear with me here—we actually addressed the root causes of our stress? I know, wild concept. We'll dive deeper into stress management techniques later in the book, but for now, remember this: your liver thanks you for not pickling it daily in the name of "stress relief."

Toxic Work Cultures: When Your Office is More Intoxicating Than a Bar

Let's face it: some work environments are about as healthy as a deep-fried stick of butter. If your workplace glorifies after-work drinking sessions or measures success by how many bottles are emptied at the company retreat, it might be time to reassess.

Remember: a toxic work culture is like a bad haircut. It's uncomfortable, embarrassing, and sometimes the best solution is to start fresh somewhere new. But don't worry, we'll cover how to navigate these tricky waters (and how to find a workplace that won't constantly test your sobriety) in later chapters.

The Truth Bomb

Here's the honest truth, served straight up: maintaining sobriety in the professional world isn't always easy. There will be challenges. There will be moments of doubt. There might even be times when you find yourself longingly eyeing the mouthwash in the office bathroom (Pro tip: don't do it).

But here's the good news: every challenge you overcome, every trigger you navigate, and every sober success you achieve is making you stronger. You're not just maintaining sobriety; you're building resilience, sharpening your mind, and setting yourself up for long-term success.

So the next time you feel overwhelmed by workplace triggers, remember this: you're not weak for feeling tempted. You're incredibly strong for resisting. And with the strategies we'll cover in this book, you'll be bench-pressing those triggers in no time.

In the next chapter, we'll dive into building a rock-solid foundation for your sober professional life. Spoiler alert: it involves more than just hiding all the hand sanitizer in your office. Stay tuned, sober warrior!

On workplace triggers:

"Triggers are like pop-up ads. Annoying, but manageable with the right tools."

Chapter 2:

Building a Strong Foundation for Sobriety (Or, How to Adult Without Alcohol)

Welcome back, sober superstar! Now that we've identified the workplace booze landmines, it's time to build your sobriety fortress. Think of it as constructing a pillow fort, but instead of pillows, we're using healthy habits and instead of keeping out imaginary monsters, we're keeping out real-life temptations. Let's dive in!

The Morning Routine: Your Secret Weapon

Remember when your morning routine consisted of nursing a hangover and praying for death? Good news! Those days are over. It's time to create a morning routine that sets you up for success.

Here's a revolutionary concept: what if you woke up... wait for it... not feeling like garbage? I know, mind-blowing. Start your day with activities that energize you. Maybe it's meditation, maybe it's a run, or maybe it's just staring at your house plant and whispering motivational quotes to it. Whatever works for you!

Pro tip: If you find yourself missing the taste of your morning Bloody Mary, try a virgin version. All the tomato juice, none of the regret!

Boundaries: Not Just for Countries Anymore

In the world of sobriety and career success, boundaries are your new best friend. Think of them as the bouncer at the club of your life, deciding what gets in and what gets kicked to the curb.

Start by setting clear work hours. Just because your boss emails you at 10 PM doesn't mean you need to respond. Unless you're a heart surgeon on call, in which case, maybe respond. For the rest of us, it can probably wait until morning.

Remember: "No" is a complete sentence. You don't need to attend every after-work happy hour or client dinner. Your sobriety is more important than Bob from accounting's karaoke rendition of "Sweet Caroline."

Self-Care: Treat Yo' Self (Sober Edition)

Self-care isn't just face masks and bubble baths (though if that's your jam, go for it). It's about taking care of your whole self - mind, body, and spirit.

Find activities that fill your cup (metaphorically, of course). Maybe it's reading a book, playing a sport, or learning to knit profanity into cute patterns. The possibilities are endless when you're not spending all your free time hugging a toilet!

Remember: Taking care of yourself isn't selfish; it's necessary. You can't pour from an empty cup, unless you're a magician, in which case, can you teach me that trick?

The Power of Routine: Boring, but Effective

Humans are creatures of habit. Unfortunately, one of those habits used to be drinking. The good news? You can create new, healthier habits!

Establish a routine that supports your sobriety. Maybe it's attending a support group meeting every week, having a standing dinner date with sober friends, or dedicating Sunday evenings to meal prep and planning for the week ahead.

Pro tip: If you find yourself missing the routine of happy hour, create a new one. "Happy Hour" can be an hour where you do something that genuinely makes you happy. Crazy concept, right?

The Truth Bomb (Part II)

Building a strong foundation for sobriety isn't always Instagram-worthy. There will be days when your morning routine consists of hitting snooze 17 times, your boundaries are as firm as a wet noodle, and your self-care looks like eating ice cream straight from the tub while watching cat videos.

And you know what? That's okay.

Remember: Progress, not perfection. Every small step you take towards building a healthier routine is a victory. Celebrate those victories! Maybe not with champagne, but you get the idea.

In the next chapter, we'll tackle the beast that is professional social situations. Spoiler alert: it involves more than just hiding in the bathroom during office parties. Stay tuned, sober socialite!

On dealing with stress without alcohol:

"Remember: The best stress relief is the one that works for you. If traditional methods aren't cutting it, don't be afraid to think outside the bottle... er, box."

Chapter 3:

Navigating Professional Social Situations (Or, How to Network Without Getting Tangled in the Open Bar)

Welcome back, sober socialite! It's time to tackle the elephant in the room – or should I say, the cocktail shaker at the networking event. Professional social situations can feel like navigating a minefield when you're sober, but fear not! By the end of this chapter, you'll be mingling like a pro, minus the liquid social lubricant.

Business Dinners: More Than Just Avoiding the Wine List

Ah, the business dinner. Where careers are made, deals are sealed, and livers are... well, no longer your concern! But how do you navigate this gastronomic gauntlet without your old friend alcohol? Let's break it down:

1. The Drink Order: When everyone else is perusing the wine list, confidently order your non-alcoholic beverage of choice. "I'll have a sparkling water with lime, please. I'm the designated driver... for my career." Boom! Self-deprecating humour: 1, Awkwardness: 0.
2. The Food Focus: Use this opportunity to really appreciate the menu. While your colleagues are three sheets to the wind, you'll be the one remembering the exquisite flavours of that truffle risotto. Plus, you'll, remember the important business discussions!
3. The Exit Strategy: Have a plan for if things get uncomfortable. "Oh, would you look at the time! I have an early morning meeting with... myself. In the gym. Gotta run!"

Remember, you're not missing out on the alcohol; you're gaining clarity, control, and the ability to expense a fancy meal without guilt. Win-win-win!

Networking Events: Sober Schmoozing 101

Networking events can feel like a special kind of torture when you're sober. All that small talk without liquid courage? Terrifying. But here's a secret: sober networking is actually your superpower. Here's why:

1. Clear Head, Sharp Memory: While others are struggling to remember names, you'll be the one with the crystal-clear recall. "Nice to see you again, Bob! How's that project you mentioned last time going?" Instant connection established.
2. Genuine Connections: Without the alcohol haze, you'll form more authentic relationships. Plus, you'll actually remember the conversations you have. Novel concept, right?

3. The Mocktail Mastermind: Get creative with your non-alcoholic drinks. A "Nojito" or a "Virgin Mary" can be great conversation starters. "What are you drinking?" "Oh, this? It's a Sobriety Sunrise. Want to try it?"

Pro tip: If you're feeling overwhelmed, it's okay to take breaks. Step outside for some fresh air, or find a quiet corner to recharge. Your sobriety is more important than making small talk with every person in the room.

Handling Peer Pressure: Just Say No (But Make It Funny)

We've all been there. The colleague who just won't take no for an answer when offering drinks. Here are some strategies to handle the peer pressure with grace (and a dash of humor):

1. The Redirect: "Thanks for the offer, but I'm actually training for a marathon. A marathon of excel spreadsheets, that is."
2. The Health Nut: "I'm on this crazy new diet. It's called 'remembering what I did last night.' It's very exclusive."
3. The Dad Joke: "I don't drink anymore. Or any less." *Ba dum tss*
4. The Honest Approach: Sometimes, honesty really is the best policy. "I appreciate the offer, but I don't drink. I'm much funnier without it, trust me."

Remember, true colleagues will respect your choices. Anyone who doesn't... well, they might just be jealous of your sparkling wit and clear complexion.

The Dreaded Office Party: Surviving and Thriving

Office parties can be a minefield of temptation and awkward moments. But with the right mindset, they can also be opportunities to shine. Here's your survival guide:

1. Be the Photographer: Volunteer to take photos. It gives you a purpose, keeps your hands busy, and provides a built-in excuse to circulate without a drink.
2. Become the Snack Connoisseur: Position yourself near the food table. You can't hold a drink if you're double-fisting those mini quiches!
3. The Early Exit: Make an appearance, mingle for a bit, then make a graceful exit. "I'd love to stay, but I have a hot date with my pillow. It gets jealous if I'm out too late."
4. Be the Designated Driver: Offer to drive colleagues home. You'll be the office hero, and you have a rock-solid excuse for not drinking.

The Truth Bomb (Part III)

Here's the reality: navigating professional social situations sober can be challenging. There will be moments of discomfort, times when you feel left out, and occasions where you question why you're putting yourself through this.

But here's the flip side: every event you navigate sober is a victory. Every genuine connection you make, every clear-headed conversation you have, every morning after where you wake up without a hangover – these are all wins.

You're not just surviving these events; you're rewriting the rules of professional socializing. And trust me, your future self (and liver) will thank you.

In the next chapter, we'll tackle the tricky topic of disclosure and privacy. Spoiler alert: it doesn't involve skywriting "I'M SOBER" above your office building. Stay tuned, you transparent trendsetter !

On the benefits of sobriety in the workplace:

"Your sobriety is making you a better professional every single day. You're present, focused, and bringing your authentic self to work. You're building genuine relationships and making clear-headed decisions."

Chapter 4:

Disclosure and Privacy (Or, To Tell or Not to Tell, That Is the Question)

Welcome back, sober secret-keeper! It's time to tackle the big question: should you tell your colleagues about your sobriety, or keep it under wraps like that embarrassing baby photo your mom threatens to show your dates? Let's dive in!

The Pros and Cons of Spilling the (Non-Alcoholic) Beans

Pros of Disclosure:

1. Authenticity: No more creative excuses for why you're not drinking.
2. Support: Colleagues might become unexpected allies in your journey.
3. Inspiration: You might inspire others who are struggling.

Cons of Disclosure:

1. Judgment: Some people might not understand (their loss!).
2. Gossip: Office gossip is real, and you might become the subject.
3. Pressure: Some might see your sobriety as a challenge to "fix."

Remember, there's no one-size-fits-all answer. Your sobriety is your business, and you get to decide who's privy to that information.

The "Sobriety Talk": Less Awkward Than "The Birds and the Bees"

If you decide to disclose, here are some ways to approach the conversation:

1. The Casual Mention: "Oh, I don't drink. Pass the sparkling water, would you?"
2. The One-on-One: Pull trusted colleagues aside for a quick chat.
3. The Email Approach: For larger groups, a brief email can do the trick.

Pro tip: Practice your disclosure with a friend or in front of a mirror. Bonus points if you can do it without breaking into nervous laughter or jazz hands.

Know Your Rights: Because Knowledge Is Power (And So Is Sobriety)

Understanding your rights and company policies is crucial. Here's a crash course:

1. ADA Protection: Alcoholism is covered under the Americans with Disabilities Act.

2. Privacy: Your health information is confidential. HR can't disclose your sobriety without your consent.
3. Reasonable Accommodations: You may be entitled to accommodations that support your sobriety.

Remember: You're not asking for special treatment; you're ensuring a fair and supportive work environment. And that's something worth toasting to (with sparkling cider, of course).

On using technology for sobriety:

"If anyone asks why you're always on your phone, just say you're 'optimizing your productivity ecosystem.' They'll either be impressed or too confused to ask follow-up questions."

Chapter 5:

Stress Management for Sober Professionals (Or, How to Chill Out Without Chilling a Bottle)

Welcome, stressed-out soberista! Remember when your stress relief came in a bottle? Well, now it's time to discover healthier (and legal) alternatives. Buckle up, because we're about to zen the heck out of your work life.

Healthy Alternatives to the After-Work Drink

1. Exercise: Swap happy hour for a happy run. Endorphins are nature's stress-busters!
2. Meditation: Find your inner peace (it's in there, we promise).
3. Hobby Time: Whether it's painting, cooking, or extreme origami, find something you love.
4. Mocktail Mixology: Get creative with non-alcoholic beverages. Virgin Piña Colada, anyone?

Remember: The best stress relief is the one that works for you. If traditional methods aren't cutting it, don't be afraid to think outside the bottle... er, box.

Mindfulness in the Workplace: Not Just for Yoga Instructors

Bringing mindfulness into your workday can be a game-changer. Here are some techniques:

1. Desk Meditation: A quick 5-minute meditation between tasks can reset your mind.
2. Mindful Breathing: Take deep breaths when you feel stressed. Bonus: It's less obvious than screaming into a pillow.
3. Gratitude Practice: List three things you're grateful for each day. Even if it's just "I'm grateful I didn't tell my boss what I really think."

Pro tip: If anyone catches you doing desk meditation, just tell them you're pondering a complex spreadsheet formula. They'll leave you alone, guaranteed.

Time Management: Because "Wine O'Clock" Is No Longer an Option

Effective time management can significantly reduce stress. Here are some strategies:

1. Prioritize: Not everything is urgent. Learn to distinguish between "ASAP" and "When you get around to it."
2. Break Tasks Down: Large projects are less overwhelming when broken into smaller steps.
3. Learn to Say No: You can't do everything. Unless you're a superhero, in which case, why are you reading this book?

Remember: Time management isn't about squeezing more work into your day. It's about making the most of your time so you can enjoy life outside of work too.

On nutrition for sober professionals: "Remember: You are what you eat. So don't be fast, cheap, or easy. Unless that's your brand, in which case, you do you."

Chapter 6:

Career Advancement While Maintaining Sobriety (Or, Climbing the Corporate Ladder Without a Liquid Safety Net)

Welcome back, sober go-getter! It's time to talk about advancing your career without the "liquid confidence" you once relied on. Spoiler alert: You're about to discover that sobriety is your career superpower!

Setting and Achieving Goals: No "Beer Goggles" Required

1. Be SMART: Set Specific, Measurable, Achievable, Relevant, and Time-bound goals.
2. Visualize Success: Picture yourself achieving your goals. Bonus: These daydreams are way better than drunk texts.
3. Celebrate Milestones: Reward yourself for progress. Treat yourself to something nice that isn't a hangover.

Remember: Your goals are valid and achievable. And the best part? You'll actually remember accomplishing them!

Building Genuine Professional Relationships: No Liquid Social Lubricant Needed

1. Active Listening: Pay attention to what others are saying. It's amazing what you can learn when you're not thinking about your next drink.
2. Follow Up: Remember details from conversations and follow up. You'll be amazed at how impressed people are when you recall their dog's name.
3. Be Authentic: Let your true personality shine. Turns out, you're pretty awesome without the alcohol mask.

Pro tip: If you're nervous about networking, remember that most people are too worried about themselves to notice if you're awkward. Embrace your inner awkward turtle!

Sobriety: Your Career Superpower

Here's why sobriety gives you a career edge:

1. Clarity: Clear mind, clear goals, clear path to success.
2. Reliability: You're the colleague who always shows up, hangover-free and ready to work.
3. Productivity: More energy and focus means more gets done.

4. Financial Savvy: The money you save on alcohol can be invested in your career development.

Remember: Your sobriety is an asset, not a liability. You're not missing out; you're gaining an edge.

The Truth Bomb (Part IV)

Career advancement while maintaining sobriety isn't always easy. There will be challenges, temptations, and moments of doubt. You might see colleagues bonding over drinks and feel left out. You might wonder if you're missing opportunities by not participating in "liquid lunches."

But here's the truth: Your sobriety is making you a better professional every single day. You're present, focused, and bringing your authentic self to work. You're building genuine relationships and making clear-headed decisions.

In the long run, these qualities will take you much further than any momentary "liquid courage" ever could. So keep pushing forward, sober superstar. Your career success story is just beginning, and it's going to be one hell of a read – one that you'll remember every detail of.

In the next chapter, we'll tackle how to handle setbacks and challenges without reaching for the bottle. Spoiler alert: It involves more ice cream than you might expect. Stay tuned, resilient warrior!

On the importance of sleep: "A good night's sleep is like a really good bra – supportive, uplifting, and essential for looking your best."

Chapter 7:

Handling Setbacks and Challenges (Or, When Life Gives You Lemons, Don't Ferment Them)

Welcome back, resilient reader! Life, much like that printer that always jams, has a way of throwing challenges at us. But fear not! We're about to master the art of bouncing back without bouncing into a bar.

Dealing with Work-Related Triggers Like a Boss

1. Identify Your Triggers: Is it stress? Celebration? That one coworker who pronounces "espresso" as "expresso"?
2. Develop Coping Strategies: Deep breathing, a quick walk, or silently judging Karen's grammar in your head.
3. Have an Exit Plan: Sometimes, the best strategy is a tactical retreat. "Sorry, I have to go... feed my pet rock."

Remember: Triggers are like pop-up ads. Annoying, but manageable with the right tools.

Coping with Career Disappointments (Without Drowning Your Sorrows)

1. Allow Yourself to Feel: It's okay to be disappointed. Cry, scream into a pillow, or aggressively reorganize your sock drawer.
2. Reframe the Situation: Every setback is a setup for a comeback. Or at least a good story for your memoir.
3. Take Action: Develop a plan to move forward. Action is the antidote to anxiety (and much healthier than tequila).

Pro tip: Ice cream is an acceptable coping mechanism. In moderation. Maybe.

Creating Your Sober Support Squad at Work

1. Find Your Allies: Look for colleagues who support your journey. They're out there, probably by the water cooler.
2. Join Support Groups: Whether in-person or online, connect with others who get it.
3. Consider a Mentor: Find someone who's walked this path before. Bonus if they have a good sense of humour.

Remember: You're not alone in this journey. Unless you're reading this book in a sensory deprivation tank. In which case, impressive multitasking!

From "The Pitch Perfect Pivot" success story in chapter 12:

"Turns out, I'm funnier, quicker, and more creative when I'm not pickling my brain. Now, I close deals with sharp wit instead of strong drinks."

Chapter 8:

Technology and Tools for Sober Professionals (Or, There's an App for That)

Welcome, tech-savvy teetotaller! In this digital age, there's more support at your fingertips than ever before. Let's explore how technology can be your sober sidekick.

Apps That Are Better Than a Bartender

1. Sobriety Trackers: Watch your sober days stack up like your unread emails.
2. Meditation Apps: Find your zen, even in the chaos of a Monday morning meeting.
3. Virtual Support Groups: Connect with others without leaving your couch. Pants optional.

Pro tip: If anyone asks why you're always on your phone, just say you're "optimizing your productivity ecosystem." They'll either be impressed or too confused to ask follow-up questions.

Online Communities That Don't Revolve Around "Wine Mom" Culture

1. Reddit's r/stopdrinking: A supportive community that understands the struggle is real.
2. LinkedIn Groups for Sober Professionals: Network and stay sober? Multitasking at its finest.
3. Facebook Support Groups: Yes, Facebook can be used for something other than stalking your ex.

Remember: The internet is like a bar – there are good spots and sketchy spots. Choose your online hangouts wisely.

Using Tech to Boost Productivity (And Not Just to Drunk Text Your Ex)

1. Time Management Apps: Because "wine o'clock" is no longer on your schedule.
2. Focus Apps: Block distractions and enter the zone. No, not the Twilight Zone.
3. Health and Fitness Trackers: Monitor your progress as you transform into a sober superhero.

Pro tip: If all else fails, turn your phone off and on again. It works for IT issues, why not life issues?

From "The Networking Ninja" success story in chapter 12:

"Now, I'm the networking ninja. Armed with seltzer and a clear head, I make meaningful connections. And the best part? I haven't tried to recruit a single ficus into my LinkedIn network since."

Chapter 9:

Physical and Mental Health for Career Success (Or, Treating Your Body Like a Temple, Not a Frat House)

Welcome, health-conscious hustler! Now that you're not poisoning yourself regularly, let's talk about treating your body and mind right. Spoiler alert: It doesn't involve a "beer and pizza" diet.

Nutrition Tips for the Busy Professional

1. Meal Prep: Sunday meal prep is the new Sunday Funday.
2. Hydrate: Water is your new best friend. Sorry, coffee, you've been demoted.
3. Balanced Diet: Aim for a rainbow on your plate. No, Skittles don't count.

Remember: You are what you eat. So don't be fast, cheap, or easy. Unless that's your brand, in which case, you do you.

Fitting Exercise Into Your Schedule (No, Reaching for the Remote Doesn't Count)

1. Desk Exercises: Impress your coworkers with your subtle desk squats.
2. Lunch Break Workouts: Swap happy hour for a happy run.
3. Standing Desk: Because sitting is the new smoking, and you're done with bad habits.

Pro tip: If anyone questions your desk exercises, just say you're "optimizing your biomechanical efficiency." They'll either be impressed or call HR.

The Importance of Sleep (And Not the Kind Induced by Passing Out)

1. Consistent Sleep Schedule: Your body loves routine more than Karen loves talking about her keto diet.
2. Create a Sleep Sanctuary: Your bedroom should be for sleep and sleep-adjacent activities only. Netflix doesn't count.
3. Wind-Down Routine: Develop a pre-sleep ritual that doesn't involve scrolling through your ex's Instagram.

Remember: A good night's sleep is like a really good bra – supportive, uplifting, and essential for looking your best.

From "The Sober Coder's Caffeine Conundrum" success story in chapter 12:

"Now, I'm the go-to problem solver in my team. I've replaced beer with La Croix, and my biggest addiction is finding unnecessarily complex solutions to simple coding problems. Hey, old habits die hard."

Chapter 10:

Long-term Career Planning for Sober Professionals (Or, Dreaming Big Without the Beer Goggles)

Welcome, future-focused friend! It's time to plan your career trajectory with a clear mind and steady hand. No more drunken declarations of "I'm gonna be a rockstar!" (unless that's actually your career goal, in which case, rock on).

Aligning Your Career with Your Values

1. Identify Your Values: What matters most to you? Besides not waking up with a hangover, of course.
2. Assess Your Current Role: Does it align with your values, or is it as misaligned as socks in a teenager's drawer?
3. Plan for Alignment: If there's a mismatch, start planning your next move. Chess, not checkers, people.

Remember: A career aligned with your values is like a perfectly tailored suit – it just feels right.

Considering Career Changes or Transitions

1. Self-Assessment: What are your skills, passions, and strengths? Besides your impressive ability to open a beer bottle with anything, of course.
2. Research: Explore potential career paths. Yes, this means actual research, not just watching "Office Space" again.
3. Skill Development: Identify gaps and start learning. The world is your oyster, and you're no longer allergic to shellfish (metaphorically speaking).

Pro tip: If you're considering a drastic career change, start small. Rome wasn't built in a day, and neither is a fulfilling career (unless you're really, really lucky).

Mentorship and Giving Back

1. Find a Mentor: Look for someone who's walked the path you want to tread. Bonus points if they have a good sense of humour.
2. Be a Mentor: Share your experience with others. Your story could be someone else's survival guide.
3. Volunteer: Give back to your community. It's good for the soul and looks great on a resume.

Remember: Success is like a good joke – it's best when shared.

From the conclusion in the next chapter:

"Now, go forth and conquer, you sober superstar! Your success story is waiting to be written. And who knows? Maybe one day, you'll be sharing your own tale of triumph in the next edition of this book. Just remember us little people when you're accepting your 'Sober Professional of the Year' award!"

Chapter 11:

Conclusion (Or, You've Made It This Far, Might As Well Finish)

Congratulations, sober superstar! You've made it to the end of this book, which is more than we can say for that kale smoothie in your fridge. Let's wrap this up with a neat little bow, shall we?

Recap of Key Strategies

1. Build a strong foundation for sobriety
2. Navigate professional social situations with grace (and humor)
3. Manage stress without liquid crutches
4. Advance your career with a clear mind and focused goals
5. Handle setbacks like a boss
6. Leverage technology to support your journey
7. Prioritize your physical and mental health
8. Plan for long-term career success

Remember: These strategies are like a good non-alcoholic beer – they work best when you actually use them.

Words of Encouragement for the Road Ahead

You've embarked on an incredible journey, one that will transform not just your career, but your entire life. There will be challenges, sure, but there will also be triumphs beyond your wildest dreams.

You're not just surviving sobriety; you're thriving in it. You're rewriting the rules of what it means to be a successful professional, and you're doing it with clarity, authenticity, and probably a lot of sparkling water.

So go forth, conquer that career ladder, and show the world what a sober, focused, slightly-caffeinated-but-in-a-healthy-way professional can do!

Additional Resources and Support Options

1. Support Groups: AA, SMART Recovery, LifeRing (because sometimes you need more than just this witty book)
2. Professional Organizations: Check out industry-specific groups for sober professionals

3. Therapy and Counseling: Because sometimes you need to talk to someone who's legally obligated to listen
4. Online Resources: Websites, forums, and blogs dedicated to sober living and career success
5. This Book: Keep it handy for those moments when you need a laugh, a strategy, or a reminder of how far you've come

Remember: Asking for help is a sign of strength, not weakness. It takes guts to admit you can't do it all alone (and let's face it, you're already pretty gutsy for getting this far).

In conclusion, dear reader, remember this: Your sobriety is your superpower. It's the secret ingredient to your success, the wind beneath your wings, the... okay, we'll stop with the cheesy metaphors. You've got this. Now go out there and show the world what a sober professional can do!

And if all else fails, remember: At least you're not hungover.

The End (Or is it just the beginning?)

Chapter 12:

Sobering Tales of Triumph (Or, How I Learned to Stop Worrying and Love the Mocktail)

Welcome to the grand finale, the pièce de résistance, the cherry on top of our sobriety sundae! In this chapter, we're diving into the real-life stories of professionals who've not only maintained their sobriety but have also climbed the career ladder with the grace of a caffeinated gazelle.

These tales come from brave souls who've battled the boardroom booze blues and lived to tell the tale. They've agreed to share their stories anonymously, proving that while they may be sober, they're not immune to a little mystery. So grab your sparkling water, settle into your ergonomic chair, and prepare to be inspired, amused, and maybe a little misty-eyed (blame it on the onions again).

1. "The Pitch Perfect Pivot"

I was known as the "closer" in my advertising agency. My secret weapon? A three-martini lunch followed by a whiskey-fuelled presentation. I thought I was Don Draper incarnate. Turns out, I was more like Don Draper's hungover cousin.

The wake-up call came when I pitched a diaper brand to a dog food company. In my defense, both products deal with... output. After that disaster, I decided to get sober. The first sober pitch was terrifying. My hands shook, but not from withdrawal - from actual nerves!

But here's the kicker: I nailed it. Turns out, I'm funnier, quicker, and more creative when I'm not pickling my brain. Now, I close deals with sharp wit instead of strong drinks. And the only thing I'm addicted to is the rush of landing a big account - and maybe the occasional overprice boutique coffee.

2. "The Networking Ninja"

Networking events were my kryptonite. I'd down glasses of liquid courage faster than you could say "synergy." One time, I got so hammered I tried to give my business card to a potted plant, convinced it was a potential client in a really convincing tree costume.

Getting sober meant relearning how to network. At first, I felt like a fish out of water - if that fish was also trying to make small talk about market trends. But I discovered something amazing: I could remember conversations the next day! No more waking up in a cold sweat, wondering if I'd promised to skydive with the CEO (true story).

Now, I'm the networking ninja. Armed with seltzer and a clear head, I make meaningful connections. And the best part? I haven't tried to recruit a single ficus into my LinkedIn network since.

3. "The Sober Coder's Caffeine Conundrum"

As a software developer, I lived on a steady diet of energy drinks and beer. Debugging? Drink. New feature launch? Drink. Tuesday? Drink. My code was as sloppy as my drinking habits.

Sobriety hit me like a stack overflow error. Suddenly, I had to face my code (and my coworkers) without a buzz. The first few weeks were rough. I'd reach for a non-existent beer can every time I hit a coding snag.

But then, something magical happened. My code got better. Like, way better. Turns out, a clear head is better at solving complex algorithms than a booze-addled one. Who knew?

Now, I'm the go-to problem solver in my team. I've replaced beer with La Croix, and my biggest addiction is finding unnecessarily complex solutions to simple coding problems. Hey, old habits die hard.

4. "The Boardroom Balancing Act"

As a high-powered executive, I thought maintaining my edge meant maintaining my blood alcohol level. Board meetings, business dinners, client golf outings - all were excuses to indulge. I was a functional alcoholic, emphasis on the 'functional'... or so I thought.

The turning point came when I showed up to an important merger negotiation still drunk from the night before. I nearly signed away our company's best assets for a bag of magic beans. (Okay, it was stock options, but they were about as valuable as magic beans.)

Getting sober was like learning to walk a tightrope without a safety net. Every meeting, every decision felt precarious. But as I found my balance, I realized I was sharper, more focused, and frankly, a better leader.

Now, I lead with clarity and purpose. The only thing I'm high on is success (and maybe the occasional sugar rush from the donuts in the break room).

5. "The Sales Savant's Sobering Success"

I was the stereotypical sales bro. My catchphrase? "Work hard, play harder." Translation: Sell by day, drink by night (and sometimes day). I thought my charm and a few drinks were all I needed to close a deal.

Rock bottom hit when I drunk-dialed a major client at 2 AM to pitch them... karaoke machines. We were a software company. Needless to say, I was fired faster than you can say "severance package."

Sobriety was my comeback tour. I had to relearn how to connect with clients without the social lubricant of alcohol. It was terrifying. But I discovered something: I was actually good at my job. Like, really good.

Now, I'm the top salesperson in my new company. My secret? Active listening, genuine relationship-building, and a wicked selection of dad jokes. Turns out, clients appreciate authenticity more than a drinking buddy. Who knew?

6. "The Sober Startup Savior"

In the startup world, I was known as the 'idea guy.' Every bender led to a new 'million-dollar idea.' Spoiler alert: Most of these ideas were garbage. My best one? A social network for pets. Yes, I was basically pitching Facebook for Fido.

Sobriety hit me like a failed Series A funding round. Suddenly, I had to face the harsh reality of my ideas without the rosé-tinted glasses. It was humbling, to say the least.

But then, something incredible happened. My ideas got better. A lot better. Without alcohol muddying my thoughts, I could focus on viable business models and actual market needs.

Now, I'm running a successful tech startup. And no, it's not a social network for pets. Though I still think Fido would love to swipe right on that cute poodle next door...

7. "The Mindful Manager's Metamorphosis"

As a project manager, I thought I needed a drink just to deal with the constant barrage of emails, deadlines, and client demands. My stress management technique? A bottle of wine and a pint of ice cream. Every. Single. Night.

Getting sober forced me to find new ways to handle stress. At first, I felt like a computer trying to run without its primary software. How do normal people relax without alcohol?

The answer, it turns out, was mindfulness. I started meditating, practicing yoga, and actually using my gym membership for more than just the sauna. The result? I became a zen master of project management.

Now, I handle curveballs with the grace of a ballet dancer and the calmness of a sloth. My team is more productive, our clients are happier, and I haven't stress-eaten a pint of ice cream in months. Though I still indulge occasionally - I'm mindful, not a robot!

8. "The Freelancer's Sober Freedom"

As a freelance graphic designer, I thought alcohol was my creative muse. I'd start my day with a mimosa (you know, for the vitamin C), transition to beer for lunch (carbs for energy, right?), and end with wine (because I'm classy like that).

My wake-up call came when I submitted a design to a children's book publisher that was more suitable for a horror novel. Turns out, booze and Photoshop don't mix.

Sobriety felt like losing my creative spark at first. How could I possibly design without my liquid inspiration? But as the fog cleared, I realized my creativity wasn't gone - it was enhanced.

Now, I produce my best work stone-cold sober. My designs are sharper, my colors more vibrant, and I haven't accidentally turned any more bunnies into nightmare fuel. Plus, my clients love that I can actually remember their design briefs. Win-win!

9. "The HR Hero's Hangover-Free Triumph"

As an HR manager, I thought I needed a drink just to survive the daily drama. Mediating conflicts, conducting performance reviews, explaining for the umpteenth time why we can't have 'Bring Your Ferret to Work Day' - it was enough to drive anyone to drink.

My rock bottom? Showing up hungover to a sensitivity training seminar and accidentally offending... well, everyone. Let's just say it's hard to promote a respectful workplace when you're hugging the trash can.

Sobriety transformed me from a walking HR violation to an actual human resources professional. I discovered that empathy, active listening, and a clear head are far more effective tools than a secret flask in my desk drawer.

Now, I navigate office politics with the skill of a diplomat and the patience of a saint. I've created a more positive work environment, reduced turnover, and finally put an end to the great 'Taco Tuesday vs. Sushi Thursday' debate of 2023. And the best part? I remember all of it.

10. "The Accountant's Sober Calculation"

I was the stereotypical stressed-out accountant during tax season. My coping mechanism? Turning my blood type to Cabernet Sauvignon. I thought I was balancing the books, but really, I was toppling them like a drunk Jenga player.

The wake-up call came when I accidentally submitted a client's tax return with a deduction for a 'home office' that was suspiciously shaped like a yacht. The IRS was not amused.

Sobriety felt like trying to do calculus without a calculator at first. How could I possibly crunch numbers without my trusty bottle opener? But as it turns out, the human brain is a pretty powerful tool when it's not pickled in pinot noir.

Now, I'm a tax-season ninja. I juggle numbers with the precision of a circus performer and the excitement of... well, an accountant. My clients' returns are spotless, my calculations are razor-sharp, and I haven't tried to deduct a single yacht since. Though I still think the IRS should consider it - have you seen the price of docking fees these days?

Conclusion: Your Story Awaits

And there you have it, folks! Ten tales of triumph, ten journeys from boozy blunders to sober success. These stories prove that not only is it possible to maintain sobriety while advancing your career, but it might just be the secret ingredient to your professional success story.

Remember, every sober professional started exactly where you are now. They faced the same fears, the same doubts, and probably the same awkward moment of realizing they don't know how to small talk without a drink in hand.

But look at them now! They're climbing career ladders, closing deals, and creating success stories - all without a drop of alcohol. And the best part? They remember every victory, every achievement, and every terrible office party karaoke performance (okay, maybe that last one isn't a plus).

So, as you continue on your sober journey, know that you're in good company. You're part of a tribe of professionals who've decided that clarity beats cocktails any day of the week.

Now, go forth and conquer, you sober superstar! Your success story is waiting to be written. And who knows? Maybe one day, you'll be sharing your own tale of triumph in the next edition of this book. Just remember us little people when you're accepting your "Sober Professional of the Year" award!

The 12 Steps: Your Career Sobriety Roadmap

Welcome, sober go-getter! You've probably heard of the 12 steps before, but did you know they're not just for church basements and Hollywood redemption arcs? That's right, these bad boys can be your secret weapon in the corporate jungle. So, grab your non-alcoholic beverage of choice, and let's turn these steps into a career sobriety elevator!

Step 1: We admitted we were powerless over alcohol - that our lives had become unmanageable.

Goal: Recognize that booze is the boss of you, and it's time for a workplace coup. **Question**: When was the last time alcohol made you feel like the intern at your own life?

Step 2: Came to believe that a Power greater than ourselves could restore us to sanity.

Goal: Find something to believe in that isn't 80 proof. **Question**: What gives you hope besides the phrase "It's 5 o'clock somewhere"?

Step 3: Made a decision to turn our will and our lives over to the care of God as we understood Him.

Goal: Hand over the reins to the Big Boss upstairs (or whatever higher power floats your boat). **Question**: If your higher power had a LinkedIn profile, what would their job title be?

Step 4: Made a searching and fearless moral inventory of ourselves.

Goal: Time for some corporate soul-searching. No resume padding allowed! **Question**: If your life were a performance review, what areas would need improvement?

Step 5: Admitted to God, to ourselves, and to another human being the exact nature of our wrongs.

Goal: Confess your sins, but maybe not to HR. **Question**: If your mistakes were a product, what would the warning label say?

Step 6: Were entirely ready to have God remove all these defects of character.

Goal: Prepare for a personality upgrade. It's like iOS, but for your soul. **Question**: If your character flaws were office supplies, which ones would you toss in the recycling bin?

Step 7: Humbly asked Him to remove our shortcomings.

Goal: Ask the universe for a personal makeover. **Question**: If your shortcomings were a bad haircut, what style would you ask for instead?

Step 8: Made a list of all persons we had harmed, and became willing to make amends to them all.

Goal: Create the world's least fun contact list. **Question**: If your list of people you've wronged was a movie genre, would it be a short film or an epic trilogy?

Step 9: Made direct amends to such people wherever possible, except when to do so would injure them or others.

Goal: Time to eat some humble pie (it pairs well with crow). **Question**: If your apologies were a product, what would be your unique selling proposition?

Step 10: Continued to take personal inventory and when we were wrong promptly admitted it.

Goal: Become your own personal auditor (way more fun than it sounds). **Question**: If your daily self-reflection was a newspaper, what would the headline be?

Step 11: Sought through prayer and meditation to improve our conscious contact with God as we understood Him, praying only for knowledge of His will for us and the power to carry that out.

Goal: Establish a direct hotline to the divine (no hold music, promise). **Question**: If your meditation practice was a phone plan, would it be pay-as-you-go or unlimited?

Step 12: Having had a spiritual awakening as the result of these steps, we tried to carry this message to alcoholics, and to practice these principles in all our affairs.

Goal: Become a sobriety influencer (hashtag blessed, hashtag sober). **Question**: If your spiritual awakening was a TED Talk, what would be its catchy title?

Remember, folks, these steps are like a corporate ladder - take them one at a time, don't look down, and before you know it, you'll be at the top wondering why you ever thought you needed a liquid safety net. Now go forth and conquer, you sober superstar!

NO….

SERIOUSLY, LETS GET MORE SERIOUS ABOUT THE 12 STEPS…..

MORE SERIOUSLY............

The Sober Professional's 12-Step Workbook

Welcome to your personal roadmap to sober success! This workbook is designed to help you navigate the 12 steps with a professional twist. Remember, Rome wasn't built in a day, and neither is a sober career. Take your time, be honest, and don't forget to pat yourself on the back for every step forward. Let's get started!

Step 1: We admitted we were powerless over alcohol - that our lives had become unmanageable.

Purpose: Recognize the impact of alcohol on your professional and personal life.

Questions:

1. Describe a time when alcohol negatively impacted your work performance.

2. How has drinking affected your professional relationships?

3. What work-related goals have been hindered by your drinking?

Step 2: Came to believe that a Power greater than ourselves could restore us to sanity.

Purpose: Identify sources of strength and support beyond yourself.

Questions:

1. What does a "Power greater than ourselves" mean to you in a professional context?

2. How could this Power help you in your career?

3. What positive changes do you hope to see in your professional life through this Power?

Step 3: Made a decision to turn our will and our lives over to the care of God as we understood Him.

Purpose: Commit to following a path of recovery and professional growth.

Questions:

1. How can surrendering control help in your professional life?

2. What aspects of your career are you willing to entrust to your Higher Power?

3. How might your decision-making process at work change with this step?

Step 4: Made a searching and fearless moral inventory of ourselves.

Purpose: Honestly evaluate your strengths, weaknesses, and behaviors in your professional life.

Questions:

1. What are your top three professional strengths?

2. What are three areas in your career that need improvement?

3. How has your drinking affected your professional ethics or decision-making?

Step 5: Admitted to God, to ourselves, and to another human being the exact nature of our wrongs.

Purpose: Take responsibility for past actions and their impact on your career.

Questions:

1. What work-related mistakes are you ready to take responsibility for?

2. How has your drinking affected your colleagues or clients?

3. What have you learned about yourself through this admission process?

Step 6: Were entirely ready to have God remove all these defects of character.

Purpose: Prepare to let go of harmful behaviors and attitudes that affect your professional life.

Questions:

1. What professional habits or attitudes are you ready to change?

2. How might your career improve if these defects were removed?

3. What fears do you have about letting go of these familiar patterns?

Step 7: Humbly asked Him to remove our shortcomings.

Purpose: Seek help in overcoming professional weaknesses and improving performance.

Questions:

1. What professional shortcomings would you like help in overcoming?

2. How can you practice humility in your workplace?

3. What steps can you take to address these shortcomings yourself?

Step 8: Made a list of all persons we had harmed, and became willing to make amends to them all.

Purpose: Identify professional relationships that need repair due to past behaviors.

Questions:

1. Who in your professional life has been negatively affected by your drinking?

2. How specifically have you harmed each person on your list?

3. What reservations do you have about making amends to these individuals?

Step 9: Made direct amends to such people wherever possible, except when to do so would injure them or others.

Purpose: Take action to repair professional relationships and rebuild trust.

Questions:

1. How do you plan to approach each person on your list?

2. What specific amends can you make in each situation?

3. Are there any situations where making amends might cause more harm? How will you handle these?

Step 10: Continued to take personal inventory and when we were wrong promptly admitted it.

Purpose: Develop a habit of self-reflection and accountability in your professional life.

Questions:

1. How can you incorporate regular self-reflection into your work routine?

2. What strategies can you use to promptly admit mistakes at work?

3. How might this practice improve your professional relationships and performance?

Step 11: Sought through prayer and meditation to improve our conscious contact with God as we understood Him, praying only for knowledge of His will for us and the power to carry that out.

Purpose: Cultivate mindfulness and seek guidance in your professional life.

Questions:

1. How can you incorporate mindfulness or meditation into your workday?

2. What does seeking guidance look like in your professional context?

3. How might improved "conscious contact" affect your career decisions and performance?

Step 12: Having had a spiritual awakening as the result of these steps, we tried to carry this message to alcoholics, and to practice these principles in all our affairs.

Purpose: Apply the principles of recovery to all aspects of your professional life and help others.

Questions:

1. How can you apply the principles you've learned through these steps to your career?

2. In what ways can you support other professionals struggling with addiction?

3. How has your perspective on your career changed through this process?

Congratulations on completing this workbook! Remember, this is a journey, not a destination. Keep this workbook handy and revisit it often. Your sober professional success story is just beginning!

www.ingramcontent.com/pod-product-compliance
Lightning Source LLC
Chambersburg PA
CBHW062228220526
45471CB00009B/3396